T0368128

Drew's Peace

Heaven Hope

BALBOA.PRESS
A DIVISION OF HAY HOUSE

Balboa Press books may be ordered through booksellers or by contacting:

· Balboa Press
A Division of Hay House
1663 Liberty Drive
Bloomington, IN 47403
www.balboapress.com
844-682-1282

Print information available on the last page.

ISBN: 979-8-7652-5772-2 (sc)
ISBN: 979-8-7652-5771-5 (e)

Library of Congress Control Number: 2024924907

Balboa Press rev. date: 11/26/2024

To Andrew

You were a gift to us right from the start
We never thought so soon we would have to part
Our bright-eyed and beautiful boy
You brought to our world twenty-two years of great joy

We cherish all the wonderful memories of you
Family gatherings, sporting events, and quiet hikes in the forest, too
We always knew when you walked in the room
Your warm smile and infectious laugh would follow soon

You had a strength and heart of gold that drew people in
A quiet intelligence and presence that made people say,
"I want to talk to him"

You loved your cars though they didn't love you
But it doesn't matter because we all do

And now as you move on to the afterlife
May your sleep be deep and filled with beautiful dreams
May you be rich with the love of all who knew you
May you feel light as the air and free as the birds
May you reunite with your grandfather
and Star who are waiting for you

And we will dream of the day when we can be there with you, too

Love,
Mom and Dad

CONTENTS

Introduction ix

Chapter 1: Andrew 1
Chapter 2: Grief 7
Chapter 3: Reality 10
Chapter 4: Survival 15
Chapter 5: The Reading 18
Chapter 6: Pictures 24
Chapter 7: Music 34
Chapter 8: Hawks 39
Chapter 9: Dimes 45
Chapter 10: Heart-shaped Stones 49

Epilogue 53

INTRODUCTION

I have never been overly religious. However, I was taught the rules of the Catholic Church from a very young age. My family did not always adhere to the rules. We attended church only on holidays and during special events such as First Communion and Confirmation. My father was not religious and therefore left our religious instruction up to our mother. My mother wanted my older sister and I to make our own choices as to the extent of our participation in religion. She raised us with love and a firm belief in God. She wanted us to always have God to turn to during life's challenges. That gift would prove to be the balm to my shattered soul when I needed it the most.

I found that I was drawn to God and prayer from a young age, and I believed in many of the church teachings. I believed in the Ten Commandments and that if you were kind and helpful to others, you would go to heaven. I felt that when we finally reached heaven and stood in front of God we wouldn't be asked, "Did you go to church every Sunday?" or "Did you eat meat on Friday?" Instead, we will be asked questions like, "What did you do in life to make the world a better place?" and "How did you help others around you with the gifts that you had been given?"

I especially believed that an individual should not consult with mediums, psychics, or spirits in general for fear of opening to Satan or demons. I remember as a child going to birthday parties and refusing scary movies and games, such as "Light as a Feather, Stiff as a Board". They would give me nightmares for days after. I tried my hardest as a child to avoid the topic of spirit existence after physical death. Unfortunately, spirit avoidance was not always possible for me as I seemed to be very sensitive to the existence of spirits as a child. The house that I grew up in was very old and stayed in the family for many generations. I had many spirit encounters in that house. Most of the experiences were benign in nature but a few scared me enough to make me hide in my bedroom closet when I was alone in the house. They included the feelings of being followed and watched (especially in the basement), doors opening and closing by themselves, or water faucets turning on and off when nobody was near them.

There was one experience in that house that terrified me, and I will never forget it. I was approximately 10 years old, and I was having a restless night of difficulty in sleeping. I ventured downstairs to my mother who had fallen asleep on one of the couches in the living room. She turned off the TV and told me to try and fall asleep on the couch across from her, and she would spend the night in the living room with me. I laid there quietly thinking about the next day's activities for quite some time. The couch that I was lying on was down the hallway from the basement door. I noticed a bright light appear next to the door as if it had moved through the door. At first, I was curious, thinking the basement light had possibly turned on by itself. Then I realized the light had morphed into the shape of a translucent person and was slowly moving towards me down the hallway. Naturally, I was terrified and proceeded to pull the blanket up to just under my eyes as I stared at the apparition in paralyzed fear. I started to silently pray fervently for God to protect me. I squeezed my eyes closed, thinking it would make the spirit disappear. I finally had the courage to open my eyes, and there standing over me was the spirit looking down at me! I noticed its hands the most as its fingers were curled on the back of the couch right above my head. I could not tell if the spirit was male or female as the face was not clear. I could make out eyes, a smile and a white vail flowing around its head. My heart was beating out of my chest, and I was paralyzed in fear. I watched the spirit move around the back of my head, and I remember thinking that it was coming to get me. It moved to the stairs and after climbing halfway, stopped to look at me again. That's all I needed to get moving. I flew off the couch and to my mother across from me. As I started to shake her awake, the spirit disappeared. I told my mother what had happened, and of course, she told me I was imagining things, or I had fallen asleep and was dreaming. I pointed out that it had gone upstairs, and I was afraid for my sister, sleeping up there alone. We then both heard footsteps walking across the upstairs bedroom above our heads. My mother went to the bottom of the stairs and called up to my sister, thinking it was her. There was no response, so my mother told me to try to go to sleep. There was no sleeping that long night as I laid there in fear. The next day at the breakfast table, my sister, out of the blue, told my mother and I that she had seen my deceased grandfather the night before. Needless to say, I was more than happy to leave that house when I grew up. However, the experience reinforced for me that prayer to God will protect me during scary situations. As a young child, I thought my prayers saved my life that night.

I continued to walk through life with ease and with the thought that a strong belief in God and prayer alone would dispose of any mishap or tragedy. I continued to often pray to God for guidance with important decisions in life and I always seemed to get an answer. On one such occasion, as a young adult, I struggled with what to study in college, and I prayed to God to show me the way. I received an answer while sitting in a college writing class. A woman came in that day explaining her profession as a speech-language pathologist. She told the class that in the field of speech pathology, a person could help others of all ages with many delays, disabilities and disorders. She gave examples of different disorders of speech, language, fluency, voice, and feeding. I sat up straighter in my chair and listened closely because this profession spoke to me as God's answer to my prayers. I immediately applied to a program and was accepted.

Life marched on with this misconception of perfect order with heartfelt prayer. I went on to receive a Bachelor of Science degree in Speech and Hearing Education, and then a Master of Science degree in Speech and Language Pathology. I was honored to become a wife to my high school sweetheart and a mother of four beautiful children. I moved through my daily routine of waking up, getting the kids off to school, working all day, and possibly attending a doctor's appointment, soccer practice, or a school event at night. I am a loving wife and mother who believes in family first, always. I am certain that there are many of you out there who can say the same.

Unfortunately, there was an unseen force that decided it was time for our family to experience a wakeup call in the reality of life. I found out that a strong belief in God and prayer does not prevent tragedy. Our lives were shattered in one moment of time in the early morning hours of a cold February day in 2021. My precious oldest son, Andrew, of just twenty-two years, passed in a car accident, throwing my life into a tailspin of horror, despair, and then grief from which I thought I would never return. Life was not perfectly aligned. My faith that God would prevent all mishaps if you prayed hard enough was a misconception. I learned that there are sometimes unpleasant challenges in life that we are forced to face and must find a way to survive for the sake of our loved ones.

How did I survive? First, I put my religious fears aside and went to see a famous psychic medium who specializes in parents who have lost children. I made it my mission to find my son's soul through reading numerous books written by psychic mediums and specialists in the field of near-death experiences. Second, I relied on my continued faith in God, even though my views about what I believe religiously and spiritually had forever altered. Third, I survived through the love and support of family and friends, especially those who have lost children themselves. I found a grief support group for parents who had lost children to be immensely helpful. Last and most importantly, I opened my heart to the acceptance of miraculous signs sent by my child from heaven to give me hope, love and light in my darkest hours. I began to write every experience of these signs in a journal that I have held dear to my heart for three years and am now choosing to share with you.

I am not an experienced writer, but I pray that the writing of this book will give other grief-stricken parents the hope that they are searching for during a similar dark time in their lives. May the beautiful heavenly signs of my son bring you just as much peace, happiness, and knowledge that our children's souls truly live on right by our sides.

Chapter 1

ANDREW

$\mathscr{F}$OR YOU TO UNDERSTAND MY loss, I believe you must come to know a few of the layers of my son's personality. How do you put into words the sum of your child and his twenty-two years of existence on this earth? Just as countless moms out there would say, he is my world. All my children make up the whole of my heart, and when one is just gone in a moment's time, there will forever be a hole in that heart.

My son, Andrew, was wide-eyed and ready to experience life from the moment of his birth. He literally raised his head and turned to his father's voice two minutes after his birth, as if to say, "There you are. The man who read to me before I was born into this world and the one who will read to me almost every night soon thereafter." From a young age, books were Andrew's world, and he would get lost in them for hours, learning as much as he could. I remember seeing him as young as two years of age pulling every book off his bookcase and sitting in the middle of them while calmly turning pages one at a time. As Andrew got older, he began to love books about space, animals, nature, and magic. He completed the entire Harry Potter book series in the second

1

grade, as he was always ahead in reading in school. He carried a book wherever he went, including the dinner table, and was often told to put his book down to listen to what we were saying. His desire to learn was evident at a very young age.

Andrew, affectionately called Drew by the people closest to him, was a whirlwind of activity. He was like a racehorse galloping through life with an impatient zest to see and do things as quickly as possible. He never crawled but instead moved effortlessly to his feet at ten months and ran at twenty months old. I remember one such occasion when Drew was just twenty-two months old. My husband had received a new engineering job in Massachusetts, so we started the long and tedious drive to move there from Texas. My parents had accompanied us to help with Drew and the entire moving process. After staying over at a hotel one night during the trip, it was time to get on the road again. Drew grabbed his grandmother's cane and, as quick as a jack rabbit, ran to the hotel door, almost making it outside alone as if to say, "Get a move on, Granny! Let's go!" He just about scared my parents to death! His impatience was evident in his driving need to be first at everything. He always seemed to manage being the first in line at an amusement park ride or the first to order ice cream before his siblings. Looking back, it was as if he knew in his very soul that his life would be short, and he wanted to experience as much as he possibly could in that brief amount of time.

Drew would pretend play with his favorite Star Wars toys, plotting scenarios of life experiences far beyond his years. He was a demanding leader at times, annoying his younger brother with orders of who was allowed to play a certain character and what problems in their pretend world those characters were to solve. Even as young as five years old, his heart was big, and he would want to be the savior rather than the villain.

He would talk to adults as if he was versed in the art of

conversation as young as eight years old. He would often call adults by their first names, and I would have to correct him to be more formal with a Mr. or Mrs. title. I can remember several times when Drew was a child and was told by his teachers and adult friends that he was an "old soul." I never really knew what that meant until years later and after much research following his passing. Through reading many books, it is my understanding that an old soul is a young person who demonstrates an empathy, maturity, and seriousness that is more typical of someone much older. This turned out to be the absolute truth in Drew's case, as he seemed wise beyond his years.

As a teen and young adult, Drew had a huge, empathetic heart and felt the need to help others, not just with material necessities but emotionally as well. I remember Drew asking me to pack an additional sandwich in his lunch for a dear friend of his who couldn't afford to bring her own lunch to school. Another time, he attended the funeral of the father of an old high school friend to give emotional support. He was fiercely protective of the people he loved. Oftentimes, he would grab the hands of his little sisters, without prompting, to help them cross a street. Drew would sometimes spend quiet nights listening to his younger brother's problems before giving advice and sit for long amounts of time next to his grandmother's hospital bed when she was very sick.

Drew had a quiet intelligence that drew people in and encouraged them to talk to him about their problems. Friends were constantly seeking him out to ask for advice. At one point, I remember Drew saying to me after a particularly long day, "I'm so tired. It's hard helping people deal with their problems." I, of course, was very protective of my children and thought of him first. I told him that he couldn't solve everyone's problems and sometimes he should let them deal with things on their own. I received an eye roll in return.

I believe that his huge, empathetic heart created an anxiety in him that led to many sleepless nights and a restlessness that he never outgrew, even as a young adult. He once told me that he could remember having a problem sleeping as young as five years of age. Drew explained that he often couldn't quiet his mind about negative things that could happen in the future. He stated that in the middle of the night, unbeknownst to his father and I, he would venture downstairs all alone. He would play with our dog, Star, to calm himself before returning to bed. Star was a constant source of love and comfort to him until she passed, and I think her death affected him more than we realized.

Drew had a boisterous personality and a ready smile whenever he walked into a room. He was drawn to friendly, humorous people and had a laugh that was infectious to others. The phone was always ringing off the wall for play dates or social events, and there were always friends at the house. He never had problems in school, always receiving the best grades and making friends easily, until the fourth grade when things changed.

Drew spent his entire fourth grade year immersed in school studies and reading books on his own. Looking back, I remember him withdrawing from wanting to play football and spending time with friends from school. At the time, I thought he was growing up and finding other interests. After all, he was at the top of his class, doing well academically. Emotionally, however, he was struggling. Reality set in when he got off the school bus one day, walked up to me, placed his head on my chest, and burst into tears. I remember feeling panicked at first, not knowing what could possibly cause my child to cry like that. Then, the anger of a protective mama bear took over when I found out why. One of his classmates, for the entire fourth grade year, would bully Drew with hurtful words every time the teacher would turn her back to the class or leave the room. She would humiliate him in front of his peers, calling out names like fatso, fat bird, nerd boy, owl eyes, teacher's pet, and a host of others that make me ill to mention. My husband immediately called the girl's parents to put a stop to this despicable behavior. I talked to the classroom teacher to make sure that she was aware of the problem. Unfortunately, the hurtful choices of a person can have profound and lasting effects on others. That year was particularly difficult for Drew, not only because of the relentless bullying but also because of the loss of his beloved grandfather to cancer and the passing of his precious dog, Star. Years later, we would come to realize the physical and emotional toll this had on him.

Drew loved nature, including animals, quiet hikes in the forest, and fishing in peaceful lakes. Some of the best times that we had as a family were quiet hikes up to waterfalls and in forests near our home. He enjoyed spending time with friends, talking, playing video games, listening to music, and, when he was a young adult, occasionally smoking marijuana. Of course, my husband and I could not understand the reasoning behind this and would urgently educate Drew on the harmful effects this habit could have on him. It took a few long and stressful years for him to finally open up to my husband and me about his behavior. He taught us the important parental lesson that love, kindness, and patience always prevail. When he finally was willing to confide in us, he explained that he was attempting to self-medicate due to overwhelming feelings of anxiety that had followed him his entire life. He also admitted to a binge eating disorder caused by his anxiety but also by the relentless body image bullying early in life. He agreed to get help. Drew's father immediately took him to a doctor who could help him with both.

After therapy, medication, and much hard work on his part, Drew seemed happy and content in the last two years of his life. He found a good job in sales, went to college to finish his degree in business, spent time with his beloved girlfriend, and grew closer to his family. He never said no to family vacations and looked forward to times when we were all together. None of us expected the tragedy that would unfold.

I can't explain why I always felt anxious when Drew left the house for an activity or time spent with friends. Looking back, I always had a picture of my other children's lives in the future and what they might be doing for a career. With Drew, it was different. I could never picture his future and what it would entail, and so I worried constantly about him. I have no idea what caused this feeling of anxiety on his behalf. Perhaps it was a premonition of what was to come. He would often say to me, "If you really believe in God, Mom, pray more and stop worrying." He even gave me a coffee mug for Christmas with the words "Pray more, worry less" printed on the front two months before he passed.

Chapter 2

GRIEF

THAT FEBRUARY NIGHT WAS COLD, with freezing rain, high winds, and black ice on the roads. It was around two a.m. in the morning when I heard the bedroom door quietly open. I opened one eye and watched Drew kneel at the foot of our bed. He gently shook his father's leg, apologized for waking us, and asked if he could borrow his dad's phone. Drew briefly explained that he was out with his friends the night before and left his phone at his girlfriend's house by accident. He was afraid that she would get anxious if she could not contact him, and he wanted to text her on his dad's phone so she knew he was okay. My husband handed Drew the phone and allowed him to text. Drew got up and walked out the bedroom door. It was the last time that my husband and I saw our son alive. We found out many hours later that his girlfriend had driven to our house early that morning to return Drew's phone, and he decided to spend the rest of the night at her house. He chose to follow her home in his own car so that he would have it for work later that day. The police couldn't say exactly what happened, but they thought maybe Drew had been driving too fast and had slid on ice or maybe fell asleep at the wheel before attempting to avoid hitting a pole. He totaled his car and died instantly.

I am sad to admit that in the moment, I was not happy when he woke us in the middle of the night. Now I see it as a missed opportunity to hug him, hold him close, and tell him that I loved him one more time. I went back to sleep that early morning thinking that I was justified in my anger and that my son was not deserving of a hug, even though I never let him leave the house without one in the past. I was only hurting myself. Instead of being proud of my son for thinking about his girlfriend's feelings and being a gentleman as my husband and I had raised him, I chose to let my ego get in the way and hold onto my anger. Regret is a horrible force that weighs heavy on the heart and is relentless in its reality. It would have been far better to forgive my son that night and bask in his love in a Drew bear hug, for that is the memory I would prefer to have. I believe that too often we are so focused on what we feel is expected and proper behavior, that we forget to live in the moment and seize opportunities that become some of life's greatest gifts.

Everything on that fateful day is burned into my brain as a horrible nightmare that was forever branded there. Hours after Drew had come in and out of our bedroom, I was woken out of a deep sleep by my husband sitting next to me on the edge of the bed. He quietly told me that the police were downstairs, Drew was in a terrible car accident, and that he was deceased. What?! What does that even mean?! I could not allow for the reality of the situation to process in my brain. I preferred to believe that I was in the midst of a nightmare and begged my husband to wake me. My husband had always prioritized protecting and taking care of me. When he looked at me with the most devastated facial expression I had ever seen, and enveloped me in an embrace, I knew in that moment that this was the truth. My husband would never lie to me. Our loving, amazing, and precious boy was gone. The shock of that knowledge was so heavy that I could barely breathe. Our lives would never be the same and our family would never be whole again.

Chapter 3

REALITY

THE NEXT TWO WEEKS WERE the darkest days of my life and full of a whirlwind of activity. There was a funeral to plan, flowers to buy, music to pick out, a grave plot and head stone to purchase, an estate to close, and family and friends to greet who we hadn't seen in years. I walked through those days as if in a dream, keeping myself busy to hold back the reality of the situation. I kept picturing Drew walking into the house, slamming the door and saying, "Hey Mom! What's happening?" Then I would think of all the times that I would yell at him for slamming the door. Funny how we perceive certain actions in life to be annoying when they really don't matter in the grand scheme of things. Why had I let such mundane instances bother me? I would give anything to hear the slam of that door again by my son. I began to question what mattered in life. Certainly kindness, unconditional love, and patience were in the forefront of my thoughts.

I had close family, my other three children, and my husband going through the same horror. I even found myself smiling and joking with them and others who came to pay respects to try and lighten the mood of the situation. It was all an act to give them some hope and light in the darkness. Inside, I felt much anger at the injustice of Drew's loss. Here was a young man who fought to overcome his personal struggles, and when he finally was happy and content, was ripped from us because of a tragic accident. Also, I could barely take care of myself, so how could I be expected to take care of others? Why should I have to give them hope when I felt there was none in this world? I hid the anger when people would hug me and say, "Everything will be okay. Drew is in a better place now." In a better place?! A better place would be right here with me and the people who love him the most!

I began to turn to the friends who sat with me in my grief, silently providing love and acceptance of my sadness without judgement and giving unwanted advice. I found out who my true friends were and learned to let those go who didn't truly understand me. On one occasion, an old soccer friend walked up to me at a game field. She politely asked me about the kids. I avoided saying anything about Drew and instead talked about the life activities of my other three children. The unavoidable happened for the first time because she asked, "How is Drew doing?" I realized in that moment that this old friend was unaware of his passing. I remember sweating profusely as I forced the words from my throat, attempting to avoid the tears that always accompanied his name and the acknowledgement of his death. She looked at me in shock with a very sad and devastated face and said, "I'm so sorry, I just can't", and walked away. The anger reared its ugly head in that moment. You just can't?! I'm the one who lost my son, and you don't even have the decency to hug me and sit with me in my pain? In those long, dark days, I felt that I was acting on a stage in some horrible, never-ending play.

There were days that I would be out running errands and could finally quiet my mind with mundane tasks. Then, the nightmare would rear its ugly head again. I have always been a magnet for strangers wanting to approach and talk to me. I've always been a friendly person who can lend and an ear to others and people sense this and talk to me out of the blue at stores, appointments, etc. I was finally asked how many children I had by a stranger for the first time. I didn't know what to say in that moment. Do I say I have three children, or do I say four and need to explain all over again about the one who I had lost? It was Drew who ended up giving me the answer to that question, months later, during a reading by a psychic medium.

By nightfall, I was exhausted and had nothing left to give to others. Every night for weeks, I would lie in my husband's arms and cry for the child who I had lost and for all the beautiful dreams I had woven around him. I missed him desperately, his beautiful smile, his infectious laugh, his big Drew bear hugs, the kisses on the top of my head, and his declarations of "I love you, Mom." There was no outrunning the grief. It was overwhelming, like a living monster, stalking to gobble you whole from the inside out and steal your breath. During those long nights, I would wonder what really happened that night in the car accident. I would replay every possible scenario as if on a loop tape and what I could have done differently. I began to question my religious beliefs and wonder if my son truly made it to heaven with God or if it even existed. I knew that he had doubts about the existence of heaven and God while alive, even though he attended Catholic schools his whole life. He would often say that he felt man had made up most rules in the religion. What if he was lost and couldn't find his way to heaven?

A new low of depression and anxiety set into my soul. I remember sitting on the edge of my bed one day, alone. It was the middle of the afternoon, and the house was quiet. The quiet moments were the hardest. Keeping busy seemed to be my saving grace as it kept my mind from spinning into desperate thoughts. When I had moments alone in that first month, I pictured Drew lost as a soul, floundering in between worlds and looking for the light of God. I began to think maybe I could go to him in death and help him to heaven if he was stuck, give him a push into the light, even if my soul was lost in the process. I would give my life for any one of my children, in a heartbeat, without thinking twice. After all, my husband would look out for my other three much-loved children, but who would look out for Drew?

I sobbed on the edge of the bed in despair that day, completely lost in my sorrow. Then, the unimaginable happened. My phone, nestled in my hand, began to spin through contacts by itself. I sat in awe wondering what was happening. The phone stopped on my best friend's name, and it was as if someone else pushed the call button. I heard her voice before I even put the phone to my ear, "Honey? Are you okay?" Something told me to confide in her my deepest desire to help my son. She talked me through my desperate thoughts that day, telling me that Drew was safe in heaven, and I was needed here for my husband and my other children. She told me that this life is a gift and only God can decide when it is my time. I have no idea who pushed the call button that day. Was it Drew, God or maybe my guardian angel? I did know deep in my soul that my friend was right. It was not my time, and it was God's way of saying Drew is okay and that I must live. God used my best friend to reach me when I needed it the most. Strange how moments of grace can happen when we least expect them.

Looking back, I believe that Drew was with me in those moments of doubt and was concerned about my loss of faith in God and heaven in my sadness. He was very persistent and determined in life to get his point across in any situation. It was through my son's persistence and determination to reach me that I started to see the light through the darkness. The loving, miraculous signs that he began to send from heaven touched my soul and restored my faith in heaven and God.

$Chapter\ 4$

SURVIVAL

$\mathcal{L}$IFE BEGAN TO WIND INTO some semblance of normalcy after all the craziness subsided, and family left to resume their own lives. We, as a family, settled into a routine that would allow us to cope with our loss. The signs from my son began to manifest while I was driving home from a late-night soccer practice with my youngest daughter. For no apparent reason, I began to sweat and became extremely anxious. My heart felt like it was going to beat right out of my chest. I had never felt that much anxiety in my life, and I was almost paralyzed by fear. There was no reason for the terror that I felt. I was safely driving down the highway and my daughter, exhausted from soccer practice, was peacefully sleeping in the seat next to me. I just felt an overwhelming need to get home as quickly as possible, so I went with it and stepped on the gas a bit more. Looking back, I think that I felt my son's overwhelming anxiety in his desire to reach me.

I ran into the house and immediately into my husband's arms, asking if everything was okay with our other three children. As I was speaking to him, my phone that I had placed on the kitchen counter at my arrival beeped, signaling a new text message. I realized that it was a text from a coworker informing me that a psychic medium who specializes in families who have lost children was having a show locally in three months and everyone was guaranteed a reading. She apologized in her text if this was too soon to contact me regarding this matter, but she felt the overwhelming need to text with the opportunity. She knew that the tickets would sell out in a matter of minutes. With my Catholic upbringing, I questioned whether this was something I should get involved in. My husband, however, did not and immediately bought two tickets for the show.

I admit that I had doubts about this medium and her validity, so I purchased her book online to read. I was determined to find out everything I could about her before I attended the show. I was intrigued by her book and the claim that she could speak to the souls of loved ones in heaven. Unfortunately, I did not receive her book in the mail right away. I still wonder to this day if that was coincidence or due to forces that were working behind the scenes leading to what happened next. My curiosity became more driven, and I decided to increase my knowledge in this controversial topic of mediumship. I began to read every book I could get my hands on written by psychic mediums and professionals in the field of near-death experiences. I read books by respected and well-known authors such as George Anderson, John Holland, Suzanne Giesemann and Maureen Hancock. These wonderful authors began to give me hope that I could find the soul of my son and communicate with him again.

Life marched on as busy as ever. I didn't notice the absence of the medium's book until weeks later when my husband was paying the bills and asked me to contact the medium via email to question why the book had not been sent. I wrote the email, locked myself in the bathroom, sobbed, and silently prayed to my son. I asked him to give me a sign that it was okay to see this medium and I prayed to God that I was not committing a sin. A few minutes later, my husband informed me that the medium had answered my email immediately. To my shock and excitement, she apologized for the book not being sent and said that one would be forthcoming in the mail immediately. She went on to write that my son was there with her at that moment and was anxious to let me know that he was okay. She offered a free, private reading for my husband and I, separate from the one for which we had bought tickets. She informed me in that email that Drew had much to say to us and he was very excited for this opportunity. We agreed immediately and set a date. Looking back, I believe my son was aware of this woman's gift and how she could help us to connect with him and hoped that it would bring us some peace.

$Chapter\ 5$

THE READING

THE READING WAS A BLESSING and covered my soul in a healing embrace that paved the way for a new outlook on life, death, and the afterlife. I will never regret speaking to this medium and since then, I have met with two other well-known mediums with similar results. My son has shown that his persistence and determination has continued in heaven and that he watches over us always in loving devotion. I threw all previous religious beliefs about not consulting with mediums out the window. How could something so beautiful that causes so much hope, joy, and peace be evil or a sin? Instead, I choose to believe that these medium experiences are a loving gift from God to help with healing on earth.

From the moment that we turned on the computer to start the virtual reading, I could feel my son's beautiful soul. I opened myself to the possibility of talking to him and was so excited that I was vibrating with an energy that surpassed anything that I had felt previously in my life. I felt lighter and happier than I had felt from before the time of his passing. I could tell where he was next to me by the hair standing on end along my body and the plugging of my ear on that side, signs that stay with me even today.

I won't use the medium's name for privacy reasons, but I will say she is a funny, loving, empathetic, compassionate, and very kind woman. This woman was truly a gift from God. She made us comfortable by joking with our son to make us laugh. She validated Drew's presence by first giving us examples of his personality and preferred activities in life. She mentioned how he enjoyed playing guitar and that his college of attendance, after his passing, gave him a business degree and placed his name on an alumni memorial. The medium told us that Drew was okay, sent his love to all and that his beloved grandfather (my father) and great grandmother (Nana to him) greeted him into heaven. My husband's grandparents also came through in the reading, expressing what a gift Drew is to them in heaven.

During the reading, Drew made it a point to stress the words, "Hugs, Mom!" The medium had no way of knowing that right before the reading I had said a Catholic nine-day Novena to St. Therese of the Little Flower. The purpose was to request help in seeing my son in a dream so I could receive a hug from him. He asked for the medium's advice on how to go about doing this as he had tried to enter my dreams without success. The medium expressed her concern that I wasn't ready because my energy was so low from grief and his was very high due to him being an old soul. The medium looked right at me and told me, Drew is sending you these words personally, "Old soul! Right, Mom?" Drew knew that I would understand that message due to numerous adults in the past saying those words exactly about him to me. The medium then explained that for Drew and me to meet in a dream, we would have to match our energies in the middle. She recommended relaxation techniques and meditation to help raise up my energy level. To this day, I practice both and it has increased my ability to sense my son's soul whenever he is close to me. I have also been blessed with a recent and beautiful dream of Drew hugging me three years after his passing. I remembered the dream fully when I awoke, down to the smell of his hair. In the dream, I remember saying to him, "I wish this is real, Drew." He simply responded, "It is, Mom."

The medium shared with us that Drew's energy was very strong, and he was well-versed in sending signs, having lived many lives in the past. She also stated that he was excited to share his job of ushering children into heaven who had passed of cancer and showing them the ropes by teaching them how to get a hold of their families on earth through signs of their continued existence.

The medium gave us undeniable proof of Drew's continued presence in our lives during the entire reading. She mentioned a very private and real experience that I had while kneeling in my closet a few days after his death. The medium said that Drew was with me when I knelt in that closet, looking at his baby pictures in a photo album. When I turned a page, I found a Valentine's Day card expressing his love for us that he had made when he was eight years old. The medium knew the exact words that I used with its discovery, "How did this get in here?" She said Drew's soul was with me in that moment and that he put that card there for me to find as he passed right before Valentine's Day. I felt in my heart that she was right, and Drew was there with me at that moment to console me.

Through the medium, Drew said that his soul was with my husband in his van while running errands. He talked about how he stood, unseen, next to my husband in our driveway, watching as he removed an expired inspection paper from the glove compartment and held it in his hand. The medium stressed several times that Drew did not want my husband driving that van anymore because it was unreliable and unsafe. Also, Drew told my husband that he would send a different van as a gift instead. Months later, my husband found the van that Drew sent him. He went to look at a van at a dealer that he was interested in, only to find out that it had been sold that morning. The salesman told my husband that another van had showed up in the lot that day that was for sale. Imagine my husband's surprise when he was told by this salesman that the van had very few miles because it was used to bring children with cancer back and forth to activities. Coincidence? I think not! Drew had mentioned in the medium reading that he helps to usher children into heaven that had passed from cancer.

Drew stressed the importance of acknowledging to strangers that I have four children when I am asked. He knew that question asked by strangers caused me great anxiety. Drew then provided me with the words to give to these strangers. The medium relayed his words to me accompanied by a laugh, "You have three children on earth and one in heaven. The best is in heaven!" How could she possibly have known the one question from strangers that caused me so much stress and anxiety. I believe that Drew was there in those moments, quietly seeking a way to give me the words for a response that would calm me and make me laugh, remembering his humor.

Drew sent us beautiful messages as validations to give to each of his siblings, information that the medium would not know. He thanked my artistic youngest daughter for a memorial cross that she painted for him and told us that she is an empath and an old soul, just like him. Drew expressed the brilliance of my oldest daughter, her thoughts about cancer research in the future, and a course that she was thinking of taking to further her knowledge in this area of study. He expressed concerns for his younger brother, saying that he was struggling with his passing. The medium said that Drew was sending his brother music to help with his grief and said, "Tell my brother to listen to the words of the songs. Let my brother just be. He will be fine. I am helping him." Drew mentioned that our dog can see him, and we could recognize when he was in the room by paying attention to the dog's behavior. To this day, we will see the dog sit and bark at the corner of the room and follow something's movement with his eyes. As soon as we acknowledge Drew's presence, the dog's strange behavior stops.

Drew knew that we had questions regarding his death and that I would replay his car accident every night while I wept. He relayed the message that he was with me during those long nights, stroking my curls and placing his face against mine to absorb my sorrow and lend me strength. The medium said that Drew was stressing the importance of not focusing on how he passed, and that we needed to let that go. He explained that we would understand why things happened when we got to heaven ourselves. It would be an "ah ha" moment. He took responsibility for the accident, even though he said it was his time to go and nothing could have changed that. Drew told us we would find hobbies that would give us peace and mentioned bike rides for his father and visits to the ocean for me. We have taken his advice from the reading and find much peace in quieting our minds during bike rides while visiting the ocean. I am not surprised that Drew recommended these hobbies of peace to my husband and me. I can remember countless times when he was little, begging to be taken up on top of a large hill nearby our home and whooping with joy as he rode his bike as fast as possible down the hill, with a big smile on his face! Also, I cherish the family vacations to the ocean where he would float in the calm waters for hours while his brother and sisters built sandcastles.

The medium told us that Drew is always with us and sees and hears everything that we say and do, sometimes more than he wishes to. He knew that there were a lot of questions surrounding his death and he wanted to put those questions to rest for us. He mentioned that people were saying that he was probably driving too fast. He admitted to driving a bit over the speed limit but not as fast as people were thinking. He went on to describe the accident in detail, from start to finish, to the medium by replaying the accident as if it was a movie in her mind. She stated that she could see the freezing rain on the windshield and the curves in the road. Drew showed her how he looked down and she thought maybe he had fallen asleep. He tried to avoid the pole when he looked back up but couldn't. He then showed his soul being thrown from his body on impact and standing next to the car in awe and confusion at first. The medium stated that Drew tried to live for us, but it was his time to go. He stated he is okay, never suffered, and is still always around us in spirit.

She said Drew referred to physics on behalf of his engineer father, who is very left-brained and sometimes found it difficult to believe that Drew's soul was still around. The medium went on to say that Drew wanted to stress: energy never dies, it just changes. He used the words, "I am not dead. I'm just different." His most important message was that he doubted the existence of God while on earth. He went on to excitedly say that there is a God in heaven and he wanted to shout it from the highest mountains! How could this medium possibly know such personal details about our family? I believe my son was truly there that day, trying to ease my sadness and give me a spark for life again.

At the end of the reading, this medium asked if I had any questions for Drew before she stopped channeling? I asked what signs he would send his family to let us know that he was around. Drew promptly replied through the medium: music, hawks, dimes, and heart-shaped rocks. Although the medium did not mention pictures during the reading as a sign from Drew, that seemed to be one of the first and primary forms of communication from him, and therefore needs to be mentioned.

Chapter 6

PICTURES

$\mathcal{D}$REW WAS WELL-VERSED IN TECHNOLOGY while alive and worked for a company that sold and marketed phones and other electronics. He would often talk to me about selling phones to elderly people who wanted a basic phone without all the bells and whistles of new technology. Drew said many people were referred to him by the elderly because they appreciated the time that he took in helping them program their contact information into their new phones. Thus, I was not surprised when he started to use a phone to get a hold of his family from the afterlife.

My mother, Drew's grandmother, had moved from New York to live with us in an in-law apartment when my father passed away fifteen years ago. Drew was very close to her and my father while growing up and at times he would visit with my mother in her apartment and check on her during the day for me while I was at work.

Just weeks after Drew's passing, his grandmother began to wake up around three in the morning to unexplained pokes on the arm, movements of chairs, a knock on the wall, or footsteps above, accompanied by faint music. She claims that she would look at the phone to see the time that she had awakened, and that is when she would receive a picture from Drew that would last for a few seconds and then fade away. At first, I thought that maybe she was dreaming and that these pictures were in her imagination because she missed him so much. Then, I shockingly realized that the majority of the sent pictures were of family events that were never mentioned to my mother, she had not attended, and she had never seen. Drew was very persistent in helping us to believe in pictures as a sign.

One of the first pictures that my mother received was on Mother's Day, shortly after Drew's passing. She told me that she received a picture of a huge bouquet of flowers at 3:30 a.m. I was hopeful that this happened, but I admit that I still had some doubt about the existence of the pictures at that time. I decided to make the best of the day, regardless of my eldest son's absence, for the sake of my other three children. I decided to take our dog for his morning walk to boost my spirits, as it was a beautiful, sunny day. I couldn't find the dog and checked all over the house, calling his name. Drew's bedroom was on the first floor of our home, and I realized that his door was slightly opened. I was curious, so I went in to investigate. That's where I found our dog sitting next to Drew's dresser. I told the dog he was silly and asked him why he was sitting in this room. Anyone who knows our little Shih Tzu dog will tell you that he is very good at communicating his wants. He looked at me, up to the top of the dresser, and back at me again. My attention was drawn to the plant on top of the dresser. I was surprised to see that one of the carnation flowers had been pulled from center of the holder and left on the front of the dresser. It looked like the flower had been placed there as it was too far from the plant and could not have fallen out of the foam wedge by itself. Our dog barked and continued to sit next to the dresser until I acknowledged the receipt of the flower by thanking Drew for the Mother's Day gift. I thought of Drew that whole day, missing him and wondering if the mysterious flower was truly left by him or if it was my imagination. I stood in front of the sink later that day, cleaning dishes. When I looked up at the window, there was a dragonfly looking in at me. I grabbed my phone to snap a picture and while zooming in, realized the dragonfly looked as if it was smiling at me! I still cherish that dragonfly picture. The beginning of my true belief in pictures as a sign from my son took hold that day.

Our expressive dog, Max.

*The dresser in Drew's room with the plant
and the carnation flower next to it.*

*The dragonfly that appeared in front of me,
smiling through the window.*

Not long after the Mother's Day picture, Drew began to use pictures of animals and objects to represent various people in our lives. The pictures foretold that something wonderful was going to happen to them or that he was with them during certain activities. He also sent pictures of gratitude for things that we had done in his memory, such as a picture of his grave with a dragonfly sitting on top after we planted bushes and flowers around his headstone and pictures of angel's wings to represent a Christmas tree ornament I bought in his memory. He also sent a picture of a pine tree two days before the tree was delivered as a sympathy gift from friends.

Drew sent pictures to let us know that he was around our home, listening to our conversations. There was one weekend when my mother-in-law came from New York to visit. My husband, mother-in-law, and I sat around the table discussing family events, work related happenings, and the daily news. We were sad to see an article written about monarch butterflies going extinct. How sad to know that in the future, children would not experience the beautiful monarch butterfly flying in a field of flowers. I expressed my concern and sadness with my loved ones that day.

It was a beautiful, warm, summer day, so we decided to take a trip to the ocean in Rhode Island and hike on a path at Beavertail State Park. As we walked down the path, I enjoyed the sunshine, salty sea air, and glimpses of the ocean through the bushes. My mother-in-law and I were surprised to see a large monarch butterfly land on my husband's back as he walked in front of us on the path! We both exclaimed, "Drew!" at the same time and laughed. I told Drew that if it was a sign from him to please fly over to a bush next to us and wait for me to get my phone out to take a picture. To our shock and excitement, the monarch butterfly flew to the bush and landed, opened its wings as far as they would go and waited for me to take a picture. I knew in my heart that it was Drew letting us know that he was nearby and heard our conversation that morning about monarch butterflies. I did not have the opportunity to share the experience with my mother as we arrived at home late that night. At 3:30 a.m. the next morning, my mother received another picture from Drew. The picture was of a butterfly to validate that he was with us that day.

The monarch butterfly that sat on a bush, on request, for a picture.

Another picture showed Drew sitting in a chair in a dome-like building, playing a guitar. My mother explained that in the picture, there were three people with their backs to the screen as if they were an audience. She thought that the back of their heads looked like Drew's grandfather, his great grandfather (Papa to Drew) and his great grandmother (Nana to Drew), all of whom had passed many years ago. Two of these were people who he told the medium had greeted him into heaven. Drew loved to play the guitar while alive. He took guitar lessons for years and participated in band concerts for charities to raise money for veterans with Post-Traumatic Stress Disorder, Toys for Tots, and Child Life Specialists at Massachusetts General Hospital. Was he letting us know that he could still participate in his favorite activities in heaven?

Drew proved that he was still as helpful from heaven as he was on earth. One of my friends texted me at night to inform me that her young son had become very ill in the hospital and the doctors were unsure of the cause or if he would get better. I told her that I would pray for him and to keep me posted of his condition throughout the long night. I immediately began to pray to God for his quick recovery and said a fervent prayer to Drew to help if possible. I began to feel the signs of my son immediately. Every hair on the left side of my body stood on end, and my left ear became plugged. I could feel my son right there with me, listening intently. I told him how much I loved the sick child and begged him to help. The next morning, I went to my mother's apartment to check on her. She told me that she had received another picture from Drew at 3:30 a.m. She said it was a picture of a lion's head. I admit that I was confused about the sign because I was unsure of the meaning. Two hours later, I received a text from my friend saying that her son miraculously came out of the illness overnight and was sitting up in bed, eating breakfast. To my shock, she said the doctor walked into the room, informed the family that he was surprised to have all negative test results, and handed her son a stuffed lion as a gift. The lion picture was sent to us by Drew as a sign that this child would be okay and to continue to have courage and faith.

Other pictures followed, coming regularly in the year after he passed, pictures of happy times for the family. I believe he wanted to tell us that he is always around us and to live life to the fullest. Drew sent pictures of my artistic daughter drawing pictures while lying on the living room floor in deep thought, pictures of me holding our dog, Max, up in the air with a big smile on my face, his little sister and I smiling and petting a puppy with great joy after a soccer game, and his other sister standing next to a tree at an art museum with the sunlight shining on her and a look of peace on her face. Drew also predicted future wonderful events in our lives, such as a picture of piano keys to represent his younger brother as he was a competitive piano player all through school. The picture was sent just before Drew's brother was given a much-desired opportunity for an internship during college. One time, it was a picture of a tiger's head to represent Drew's sister's exciting college trip to Africa just before she left on her adventure.

The pictures began to slowly dwindle as we began to feel hope again and heal as a family. The pictures still appeared for two years after Drew passed, when it was a direct request from a family member or a special occasion to show us that he was still watching over the family. Examples included pictures of bouquets of flowers on birthdays and anniversaries and a picture of Drew kneeling in front of my favorite chair in prayer the day after I had a breast surgery. I began to get a bit anxious about the loss of pictures when Drew's grandmother told me that the phone company was no longer providing service to her old phone. She was told that she would have to get a new phone and we both panicked that Drew might not be able to reach us. Unbeknownst to my mother, I prayed to Drew that night and begged him to still send me pictures somehow on my mom's new phone. The next morning, I went downstairs to see my mom and she excitedly informed me that she had received another picture from Drew early that morning. The picture was a bouquet of colorful daisies. I looked up the spiritual meaning of daisies and found that they represent new beginnings, love, joy, spiritual faith, and the eternal pure life of the soul. Celtic legends describe daisies as being sent by God to parents who have lost children to comfort them. I believed Drew was telling me that he was aware of my sorrow, to have faith that he will always be around and will find a way to get through to me.

The daisy flower seemed to be a favorite of Drew's, and he sent pictures of daisy bouquets often. The day before Father's Day, I prayed to Drew that he would send a sign that he was around for his dad. My mother reported receiving a picture at 3:30 a.m. on Father's Day of a large bouquet of white daisies. I'm not sure if my husband believed the receiving of this picture. He didn't say, as he has always been polite and careful of the feelings of others. He lacked enthusiasm after I told him about the picture and seemed sad. I think he believed that my mom might be making the picture up to make him happy. Drew, however, in his determination, was not giving up on his dad believing in him. I took our dog for a walk that morning. It was a gorgeous spring morning with clear blue skies and warm weather. There was a strip of grass down the street from our house that our dog loved to walk near, and he pulled me in that direction. I was not paying attention as I was thinking of the day's planned events with my children for Father's Day. The dog had other ideas and was quite intent on gaining my attention. He stopped, sat on the sidewalk and would not move. I tried tugging on the leash and finally turned and exclaimed angrily, "What is your problem?" I was shocked to see our dog sitting next to one small patch of white daisies growing on that long strip of grass! I had walked that strip of lawn for years and had never seen daisies growing there! I believe Drew told our dog to stay there to get my attention on those daisies that day. I picked one and took it to my husband that morning for Father's Day as a gift from his son in heaven. It made him smile. The actual daisy flower was a validation of the picture. I have walked on that strip of grass almost every day in the spring since that Father's Day and I have yet to see another daisy growing there.

*The patch of daisies that appeared in a long
strip of grass on Father's Day.*

The week leading up to Drew's birthday every year is very difficult for me. I said a nine-day Novena to the Virgin Mary asking for her to go to Drew and give him a big hug from me on what would have been his twenty-fourth birthday. My mother again received a picture on her phone one week after his birthday. She said she was confused about the meaning of the picture because she was unaware that I had been saying the Novena. She explained that the picture was of him sitting in a chair at our kitchen table, with a big smile on his face, surrounded by roses of all different colors. The rose has been known to be one of the most common signs associated with the Virgin Mary. I believe that Drew received that blessed hug from the Virgin Mary, and he was letting me know that my prayers were answered. This further increased my faith in God and heaven.

Chapter 7

MUSIC

$\mathcal{D}$REW LOVED TO LISTEN TO music and would often do so late at night when he was anxious and found it difficult to sleep. Many nights after he passed, I would wake up around three in the morning and hear faint music playing along with an occasional chair moving down in our dining room. I would ask my other children if they had gotten up during the night and played music. They would look at me funny and tell me they had slept soundly and didn't have any knowledge of what I was talking about. I believe that it was Drew letting me know he was around.

Drew began to send songs through the radio to family and close family friends to give us important messages. The songs were astounding in their synchronicity. I remember one occasion, when I was sitting in a restaurant parking lot, waiting for my youngest daughter to finish socializing with her friends. A car pulled up and parked right next to my car. Out of the car stepped a young man that looked exactly like Drew. He had the same build, haircut, and favorite clothing that my son wore. I literally opened the door of my car to go to him. As I proceeded to exit the car, I realized how silly I was being. This could not be Drew.

Drew was gone. I climbed back into my car, shut the door, and cried my heart out. After a few minutes, I realized that I had to get myself together for the sake of my daughter because I wanted to spare her of my sadness. I had always kept my car radio tuned into a generic rock station. However, that day, I turned on the radio and to my surprise, on came a Christian radio network called K-Love. I had never heard of this station and therefore had no idea that they played contemporary Christian music. The song "Weary Traveler", by Jordan St. Cyr, began to play and comforted me with an important message that was given to me that day by my son. I believe he knew that I was struggling with his death and wanted to let me know that he was with me in that moment. The song provided hope that one day, I would see Drew again in heaven. The message told me to keep moving through life with the knowledge that I am never alone. The perfect song came on in the moment that I needed the strength and encouragement the most. Those song lyrics spoke to my heart and gave me hope.

From then on, I continued to listen to the K-Love radio station and Drew would send me that song when I talked to him. At one point, I remember talking to Drew on my way to work the morning after I had seen the same psychic medium at another event. I told Drew that I was proud of him for coming through and sending more messages to his family. I spoke to him about religion and how my beliefs had changed. I told him that I still have a strong faith in God because of his signs and that I agreed with him about most religious rules being made by man rather than God. I believe that God gives his love freely, no matter what we do in life. I also asked him for forgiveness if I pushed the Catholic religion on him too much when he was a child by sending him to Catholic schools. The K-Love radio host was speaking about the show's events when suddenly, the song "Weary Traveler" began to play over him while he was speaking.

The radio show host briefly expressed his shock at the playing of the song but said he would let it play because there must be a good reason. My fist shot into the air! I told Drew that was an amazing validation of his presence.

The validations of his presence kept coming through the song "Weary Traveler" just for me and became very humorous as Drew loved to joke while alive. One day, I stopped at work to drop off papers about seven months after he had passed. A coworker happened to walk into the room. She asked me how I was doing and expressed her sympathy for the loss of Drew. I told her that he is always around and began to tell her of some of the signs that my family had received. Just then, the paper shredder in the corner of the room went on by itself. The coworker was shocked and excitedly explained to me that the shredder had been broken for a couple of months and was not even plugged into the wall! We both joked and exclaimed, "Hi Drew!" To our delight, the shredder went off again by itself. We squealed like little children. Another coworker showed up to see what all the fuss and excitement was about, so we explained that we thought Drew was playing a joke on us with the starting up of the shredder. To validate our suggestion, Drew started up the shredder yet again! I was very happy when I left the office that day and even happier when I got into the car, turned on the radio, and the song "Weary Traveler" was playing. It was yet another validation of his presence.

The day before my birthday in June of the year that Drew passed, my mother received another picture on her phone at 3:30 a.m. She said that it was a picture of a vintage cameo and in the middle of the piece of jewelry was a picture of me. I believe Drew was sending me a happy birthday sign. To further validate his presence that day, he sent me the song "Weary Traveler" again when I got into the car and turned on the radio on the way to work. I was so happy to know that he was around, but I was also very sad that he could not be with me, and I told him that I missed him desperately and would give anything to go to heaven and hug him one more time. As I approached the end of my street, a cardinal flew in front of my car and the song, "God's Not Done with You", by Tauren Wells, began to play on the K- Love radio station. It was a beautiful message from my son as the words touched me deeply and I realized that it was not my time to visit heaven yet. I still had much to accomplish in my life.

Often, when my husband and I were in the car together running errands, we would get the consecutive playing of the songs, "Memories" by Maroon 5, followed by "Don't Stop Believing" by Journey. There was one night when my mother-in-law, husband, and I drove my youngest daughter to her friend's house. We smiled at each other when the two songs consecutively played on the way there. I think it was particularly important to Drew that we knew he was with us that night. We dropped my daughter off and went for a nice dinner on the water. On the way back home, I felt a hand on the side of my head push my head towards my husband and a voice say, "Stay there." Right after, we were hit from behind by another car going well over the speed limit. Our car was totaled as it spun, flipped, and fell into a ditch. I happened to be on the passenger side of the car that fell into the ditch that night and bore the brunt of shattered glass from the passenger window. Was it Drew that pushed my head to the side to protect me? Luckily, we were all okay that night. One week after the car accident, two of my long-time friends called to excitedly inform me that they had attended a show held by the same psychic medium that my husband and I met with right after Drew's passing. They both said as soon as the reading started, the medium described a soul being present as a young man in his early twenties, saying he had passed in a car accident. My friend raised her hand to take ownership and said she thought that the message was supposed to be for my husband and me. This medium remembered us and told her it was Drew and he wanted to take ownership of saving us in the car crash! He said that I had saved him many times in the past and it was his turn. It was another amazing validation from my son.

Drew often sends music to family and close friends of the family to encourage and provide hope. My oldest daughter began to apply to veterinary medicine schools. She was anxious that she might not be accepted into a program because it is so hard to get in, regardless of wonderful grades and animal experience. At the time, she began to volunteer at our local veterinary office for additional experience. She said that our veterinarian had no idea that she had doubts about being accepted and that she had never mentioned her deceased brother sending specific songs to communicate from heaven. She was observing a surgery with the local veterinarian one day and suddenly, he looked at and pointed to her and sang the words, "Don't stop believing." She told me that at first, she was shocked, but then the words touched her deeply because she believed them to be a sign from Drew. She felt like he was giving her hope and courage to become a veterinarian.

While driving to my youngest daughter's high school soccer game, "Memories" played on the radio and reminded me of Drew. I asked him in prayer if he would be attending his little sister's game? I told him I hoped he was still happy and at peace. A truck pulled in front of me at that moment and to my surprise, there was a blue dragonfly painted on the back. After I saw the dragonfly, I exclaimed out loud, "No way!" and the song switched to "Don't Stop Believing". The color blue was Drew's favorite, so I was not surprised to see a blue dragonfly on that truck. Later, I looked up the spiritual meaning of a blue dragonfly and it stands for wisdom, knowledge, transformation, and spiritual growth. I felt like this was further validation that Drew hears my prayers, and he strives to make me aware of his presence always.

Chapter 8

HAWKS

DURING THE INITIAL READING WITH the psychic medium, Drew expressed his desire to come to us as a hawk or eagle. He told her that he preferred large birds over smaller ones. During our second reading with the same medium, I held Drew's favorite sweatshirt. I hoped it would help him to come through for us with messages of love. The sweatshirt happened to be face-down in my lap with no picture showing. The medium kept saying that Drew was showing her an eagle and she wasn't sure of the meaning. My husband and I were confused and didn't know what she was talking about. Suddenly the medium told us she understood the meaning and pointed to the sweatshirt in my lap. She told us that Drew was claiming ownership of the sweatshirt and when I held it up, we both laughed because we realized there was an eagle printed on the front of it! Drew then told the medium that he would visit us as an eagle. He was true to his word. That Christmas, a young and rare Steller's Sea Eagle, a native to Asia and Eastern Russia, flew thousands of miles to near where my husband and I live. As I was crossing the bridge one day, making my way home from work, that same eagle dove right in front of the windshield of my car. The bird was huge and breathtaking in its appearance. I thanked Drew in prayer that day for such a spectacular sign. We continue to this day to see eagles and hawks circle over our heads, perch on poles nearby, or dive bomb our car as we are driving. Hawks, especially, have become a clear sign that Drew is nearby.

From the time of Drew's passing, he seemed determined to let us know that he was around. Five months after we lost him, our family decided to take an annual trip to New York to visit with my mother-in-law. Drew always loved our trips to his grandmother's house because he got to visit his favorite places while there and be spoiled by his grandmother. The morning that we were supposed to leave, the smoke detector in our upstairs hallway turned on, beeped twice, and then went off. My husband was frustrated because something always seemed to happen that he needed to address before a major vacation. We both agreed to get up, fix the smoke detector and hopefully encourage our children to get on the road early to start our vacation.

My husband and I opened the door to our bedroom and standing in front of us was a wispy, smokey figure in the shape of a man. I immediately knew it was my son, who had set off the smoke detector with his strong energy and was making his presence known at the start of our vacation. I was amazed and reached for him saying, "Hi Drew", to acknowledge him. The wispy cloud disappeared. From that moment on, we started to see hawks as a sign from Drew. As we drove the five hours to my mother-in-law's house, a hawk flew next to the car for quite some time during the journey. We saw hawk symbols everywhere, such as a large hawk statue built from metal sitting outside of a store that we passed. Also, we decided to stop at a local coffee shop in Ithaca, NY, during a planned day trip and right next to the only available parking spot was a huge, painted hawk mural on the side of the building. Next, we went to hike up to Taughannock Falls and found hawks in every shape and size nesting on the side of the falls, flying over our heads and landing on rocks next to us. We had visited the falls numerous years in the past and had never seen that many hawks. To further validate his presence that day, Drew sent us a black moth that followed us along the falls and perched on each of our family member's fingers, one at a time. At one point, I asked Drew to make the moth sit on a rock nearby so that I could take a picture. The moth complied and then perched again on my finger the entire way back to our car. As we approached the car, I told Drew that it was okay to leave us and sent my love to him. The moth flew away.

The moth that sat on a finger of each family member one at a time.

The same moth that sat on a rock for a picture, on request.

Family and friends were constantly sending me texts to inform us of their belief that Drew's soul was close by in the form of a hawk. We were sent pictures of hawks landing on posts near these friends and family members. While attending my mother's funeral in New York, my mother-in-law saw a hawk perched on a pole right next to her house where we were staying. We all believed Drew was allowing us to see his presence to comfort us in our sorrow. My brother-in-law sat by his pool one day and said a hawk landed on his fence right next to him. A close family friend mentioned a hawk sitting on a post right next to a bench that she was seated on at the airport. My daughter described a hawk landing on a fence right near her as she was walking to a college class, and she knew in her heart that it was her brother in the way the bird followed her with its eyes. My younger daughter sees hawks fly in circles over her head or perch on poles next to the field at soccer games.

The hawk that perched on a post next to my mother-in-law's house the day of my mother's funeral.

My husband and I often go to the ocean to replenish our energy and to find peace in the chaos of life. During one of these ocean visits, we were relaxing on a bench and taking in the beautiful sites of the boats. We always see seagulls flying over the waters to fish, but we had never seen a hawk at the ocean. On that day, we were excited to see a huge hawk fly right in front of us, face us and spread its wings. We watched as the hawk flapped its wings for a few minutes while looking at us, then dove to retrieve a fish from the water before flying away. My husband and I will sometimes also seek peace while on the back porch of our home, listening to music and enjoying the solitude of our backyard. We will see a hawk circle three times over our heads or an occasional cardinal sitting in a tree next to us. We consider these moments a hello from our son in heaven.

The hawk captured circling overhead while my husband and I relaxed on our back porch.

Chapter 9

DIMES

$\mathscr{W}$E WERE TOLD IN THE medium's reading to look for dimes as a sign that Drew is nearby. I began to receive dimes in odd places about ten months after he passed. One day, I went home from work to have lunch. I always entered the house from the garage door after parking my car in the garage. On this day, I opened the door, removed my shoes and left them next to the door for when I had to leave again. There was nothing in front of the door that afternoon when I walked in. I enjoyed a peaceful lunch and went to put on my shoes to return to work. There, sitting perfectly placed, heads up, in front of the door, was a shiny new dime. I knew immediately it was a sign of Drew's presence. I told him I loved him and thanked him for the dime. I opened the garage door and went to my car, and there, sitting in front of the driver's side door, perfectly placed in the middle with heads up, was another dime! I laughed in delight and told Drew that he was awesome for the amount of validations that he gives his family. The garage door proceeded to close by itself in response!

I began to wonder if Drew would listen to directives as he didn't particularly like to be told what to do while alive. I decided to try, and so one day, I asked Drew to please move a dime to somewhere that I would notice without question. Three days later, when I awoke one morning, I found a dime sitting on top of his pillow next to my bed. The dime had the year of Drew's passing, 2021, printed on it. I would sometimes hug that pillow at night to fall asleep because it still had the scent of him on it. I was excited to see the dime and immediately thanked him and took a picture of the wonderful answer to my prayer.

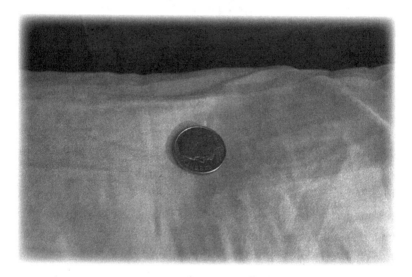

The dime found on Drew's pillow.

It was time for my oldest daughter to return to college, so my husband and I packed the van and drove back with her to help with the move. I would often say the Rosary and pray for peace and happiness for my son during long car trips. This long ride was not any different, and I talked to Drew as if he was sitting in the van right next to me. I sent my wishes for much love and peace and asked him if he would be with us while moving his sister back into her college apartment. When we arrived at the college, we all climbed the stairs to my daughter's second floor apartment. My husband touched my shoulder, said my name and pointed to the floor in front of the apartment door. There, sitting on the floor, heads up, perfectly placed in front of the door, was a dime. We both new that it was a sign from Drew.

Around two years after Drew passed, the signs from him began to dwindle. I was happy to know that he didn't feel the need to constantly leave us signs as we were living life again. However, grief is a powerful thing and at times, it creeps up on you when least expected, and those signs were a lifeline for family and close friends. One morning, my mother told me that she had gone to the local grocery store. She said that the young man at the counter looked exactly like Drew, and it made her very sad. As she told the story, it brought back memories of him, and I expressed my sadness to my son through prayer. That afternoon, I went to let my mom's dog out and to check on her after our sad conversation that morning. I noticed a dime had been left by my son, perfectly placed heads-up in front of my mom's apartment door.

When I turned fifty years old, I was told by my primary care physician to get the shingles vaccine as a precaution due to my age. I agreed and my husband and I received the vaccine on the same day. My husband was fine, but unfortunately, I had a severe reaction and became very sick the next day. The entire left side of my body was hot to the touch and felt like it was on fire, and I had a high fever. I was very frightened, and I asked Drew to watch over me that long day and night. I told him that I loved him and wanted to see him, but I needed to stay here on earth to take care of his father and three siblings. I felt better after a night of rest and decided to go to work the next day. I got up to get dressed, and sitting in between the open closet doors was a heads-up dime. I believe Drew stayed with me that night to watch over me.

Recently, I went through reconstructive foot surgery, and I have been receiving physical therapy. On one day, I walked into the physical therapy office and proceeded to the table where the physical therapist always taped my foot. I looked down and there sat a shiny, new dime, heads up on the floor. I was surprised at finding the dime there as I had not spoken to my deceased son that day. When I gasped in awe, the physical therapist asked me what was wrong. I explained that I received dimes from my son as a sign that he was around me, but I was unsure of the meaning of this one. The physical therapist smiled and said he went to pick up the dime right before I had walked in the door, but something told him to leave it. He handed me the dime and said it was meant for me. I was shocked to see the year 2021 on the dime, the year my son passed in the car accident. I found out the meaning of that dime two hours later. Drew was warning me of a sad time coming regarding his precious grandmother, to whom he always sent phone pictures. I received a call from the nursing care facility where my mother was receiving physical therapy after a long stay at a hospital. My mom had been taken back to the hospital in respiratory distress due to contracting COVID at the nursing home. She passed the next day at the hospital as she was too weak to fight off the illness. I believe Drew was telling me that he was going to be there for her when she passed and that my loved ones in heaven would take care of her.

Dime with 2021, the year Drew passed, printed on it.

Chapter 10

HEART-SHAPED STONES

THE FIRST TWO MONTHS AFTER Drew's passing, I visited his grave often during the week. I didn't want him to be forgotten, and I felt like everyone expected us to just move on with life and put our grief behind us. Unfortunately, grief does not work that way and always circles around and comes back to haunt us in the oddest of times. In the quiet moments of these visits, I would offer prayers of love and gratitude for the twenty-two years that I was blessed with my son's presence in my life. It was overwhelmingly sad to look at a grave with a dirt patch that was supposed to represent my son. I longed for the gravestone so that I could plant beautiful bushes and flowers to represent the wonderful life that he had lived. One of the first signs that Drew sent to me was three weeks after he passed, in the form of a heart-shaped stone, and was before I had even attended the meeting with the psychic medium.

It was a particularly beautiful day with a cloudless blue sky and crisp fresh air. I decided to visit Drew's grave before work that day and started the drive, knowing that tears would probably follow when I arrived to see the lack of gravestone and the dirt patch. I parked the car and stood in front of his grave. Sitting in the middle of the dirt patch was a heart-shaped stone. I was puzzled and wondered who put the stone there. I began to ask all my family and friends of Drew if they had left the heart-shaped stone on his grave. Nobody would take ownership of the stone or knew anything about it. It was only after our visit to the medium that I began to suspect that the stone was a gift from Drew. It was one of the signs that the medium mentioned that he would give to his family.

Several months after the first stone was found, we received another heart-shaped stone sign. My husband, mother-in-law, and I went to my youngest daughter's soccer game. While my husband talked to the other parents at the field, my mother-in-law and I decided to walk around the track to get some exercise. We had completed two cycles around the track in the same lane. The third time that we rounded the track, sitting right in the center of my track lane and facing me, was a heart-shaped stone. My mother-in-law and I gasped in surprise. There were no stones in sight around that field, only grass. She told me to pick up the stone as she believed that it was a sign from Drew.

The last heart-shaped stones that I was blessed to receive from my son came during a trip to the ocean. Trips to the ocean were always peaceful and rejuvenating for my husband and I and we continue to go often to this day. During one of these day trips, my husband and I decided to take a walk down the beach, hand in hand. At one point, we stopped to sit by the water and breathe in the salty air. I decided to write a message to Drew in the sand and so I took a branch and wrote, "Fly high, Drew! We love you." Those were the same words painted on a cross by my youngest daughter in memory of her brother. I believe that our son was with us that day and received the message. We started to walk back down the beach, and my husband tugged on my hand and pointed to the sand. There, sitting side by side directly in front of us, were two heart-shaped stones.

Two heart-shaped rocks in the sand.

EPILOGUE

My intention in writing this book was not to change your spiritual or religious beliefs. Instead, I hope I can inspire you to consider the possibility of another dimension where our loved ones who have passed are happily at peace and can visit and communicate with us whenever they feel the need. I first became aware of the possibility of the communication by souls in heaven during my son's funeral. To my surprise, the Catholic priest, while delivering Drew's eulogy, mentioned to look for signs that Drew would send us to show his continued existence. He said these signs would bring us hope and increase our faith in God. The priest was right, because Drew's numerous signs have increased my faith immensely. Although I no longer refer to myself as a Catholic, I have become a very spiritual person. I believe in God and that we will all be reunited with people who we know and love after death. How could I not believe after all the beautiful proof that my son has provided? When we die, none of us really knows what we will find when we step through the door into this other world until we experience it ourselves. It is my choice to call this world heaven. You may choose to call it what you wish. I like to believe that it is a glorious and beautiful place, full of unconditional love and peace, far different than anything we can experience here on earth and that our children are loved and protected there until we can see them again. Of course, I hope for the best for my child.

I will not lie; the loss of a child is by far one of the worst experiences that you will ever have to face in your life. Life will forever be different, and you will have to learn to navigate a world forever changed by the loss. It leaves a permanent hole felt by all who knew and loved that child. I understand this in a way that no amount of schooling could ever teach, only the experience itself. I can also say that in time, after acceptance and great patience, comes some joy and laughter in life's experiences again. Life will never be the same but that does not mean that it can't be filled with hope, peace, and joy if you're open to the possibility. I truly believe that is what our children want for us. The pictures that Drew sent us the most were the ones that showed us experiencing happiness and a zest for life. People have said numerous times that I am strong for having gotten through the loss. I say to them that it is not about strength, it is about not having a choice. God is not done with me yet. I have more lessons to learn, and I have other people whom I love that I must stay here and take care of.

Many people have encouraged me in the past three years to write this book in hopes that the amazing signs from Drew might help others. I know there are many people out there who will not believe these signs and will think poorly of me. In fear, I kept a lot of these signs to myself and wrote them in a journal instead, for years, to keep them close to my heart. It was Drew who changed my thought process and encouraged me to write this book. I think he can see the bigger picture from heaven and how our choices, if we let them, can have an everlasting, positive impact on the lives of others. His encouragement came in a recent reading by a psychic medium given to me as a gift by one of my dearest friends. The medium had no way of knowing that I was contemplating writing this book or that I had asked Drew for permission in prayer. At the end of the reading, Drew simply relayed the important message, "The book is a good idea. It will help many people."

My desire is that some of the signs from my son will sit as truth for you in your soul and give you hope. Whatever does not touch you, throw aside and focus only on the positive. I believe that we have a choice in this life as to whether we learn something from these negative experiences or wallow in self-pity until it eats us from the inside out and corrupts our souls. I have learned so much from the loss of my son and his signs after passing. I no longer have anger. I have found great peace and acceptance in the knowledge that Drew's beautiful soul is lovingly guiding me through this life for as long as I am blessed to be here. Finding out that love survives death is his greatest gift to me.

I have chosen to focus on positive lessons learned from the experience instead of the negative loss of life. My soul has grown significantly. I have learned great tolerance and compassion for others, forgiveness no matter the transgression, unconditional love towards all, hope amidst despair, and abounding faith. My son's passing has made my family closer than I feel they would have been otherwise. We as a family cherish every moment together now and take nothing for granted. Every declaration of love and hug is treasured far beyond any material gift. We have learned to live in the moment and to put aside society's expectations of behavior. Instead, we choose to grab moments that will lead to life's greatest gifts regardless of how silly they seem to others. I have learned who my true friends are as they have supported me through one of the darkest times in my life and have never left my side. I have been blessed in opportunities to provide emotional support for other parents going through the loss of a child.

I will always grieve for my child and think of him every day. Look for the miraculous signs that your loved ones send to you to bring light, love, and laughter to your world. I have lost my son on this earth in body, but I have found his soul in the cry of a hawk circling overhead, the quiet paths I've walked with the butterfly leading the way, the heart-shaped rocks nestled in the warm sand of the beach, and the beauty of a dragonfly smiling at me through the window. Acknowledge these signs and more signs will follow in synchronicity. Open your heart and mind to the possibility of another world and through signs, it will become more real to you than you could ever imagine. Find peace in the knowledge that your loved one's souls truly live on, right by your side.

Printed in the United States
by Baker & Taylor Publisher Services